THE BEARDED COLLIE

THE BEARDED COLLIE

By

G. O. WILLISON

FOYLES HANDBOOKS
LONDON

ISBN 0 7071 0611 7

First published 1971
Reprinted 1973
Revised edition 1977
Reprinted 1982
Reprinted 1987

© *W. & G. Foyle Ltd. 1971*

Published in Great Britain by
W. & G. Foyle Ltd.,
125 Charing Cross Road,
London WC2H 0EB

Printed and bound in Great Britain
at The Bath Press, Avon

Contents

	FOREWORD	
1	THE ORIGIN OF THE BREED	9
2	DESCRIPTION AND STANDARD	12
3	THE REVIVAL OF THE BREED	18
4	BUYING YOUR FIRST PUPPY	29
5	THE WELFARE OF THE BEARDED COLLIE	32
6	PREPARING FOR SHOW	37
7	MATING AND WHELPING	40
8	YOUR FIRST LITTER	43
9	THE STUD DOG	47
10	COLOUR IN BEARDIES	49
11	FIRST AID IN THE KENNEL	51
12	SELLING YOUR STOCK AND EXPORTING	54
13	BEARDED COLLIE CLUBS	56
14	THE KENNEL CLUB	58
15	EARLY TRAINING FOR A YOUNG PUPPY	61

Foreword

TO BE ASKED to write a foreword for a book is always flattering. In this case, however, modesty compels the admission that the choice was dictated principally because I had the good fortune to judge the first show of the comparatively recently formed Bearded Collie Club.

That request also flattered the ego. But that's another, and longer, story!

When the foreword is for the first-ever book on a breed, the pleasure is heightened.

But again, reason points out that this honour should have gone to somebody else, for the simple reason that the first breed book should have been written long before I was born!

Bearded Collies are not new. It is simply that they were lost and then mercifully re-found. Indeed they were only 'lost' because they worked in the comparative obscurity of the Scottish Highlands while other more forceful canines paraded in the haunts of the fashionable.

There was a time when Beardies were known as Highland Collies. It was a good and descriptive name for them.

Hutchinson's Encyclopaedia of Dogs certainly refers to them by that name and suggests they may have existed at the time of the Roman invasion.

More important, Robert Leighton's Book of the Dog (1907) refers to them repeatedly as Highland Collies and produces a photograph of Lord Arthur Cecil's 'Ben', a dog who would not be outclassed on the show bench today.

And as further evidence of their age (even if it does not

The Bearded Collie

take us back to Roman times!) is the portrait in the Sportsman's Cabinet (1803) of a heavily-coated Collie markedly different from the others pictured by virtue of his coat and longer ears hanging down and close to the cheeks.

One early writer describes the Bearded Collie's head as similar to that of a Dandie Dinmont. Reluctantly I disagree. Since with a dog expression is everything, surely the closest affinity is with the Scottish Deerhound?

Both have that dreamy, wistful, far-away gaze. A gentleness. And yet a nobility which lifts them out of the rut they might otherwise fall into as mere shaggy dogs.

Finally a confession. A luxury which no judge should permit himself. Before making it I insist that the writer has yet to be born who can create a perfect word picture of a dog.

Equally no artist exists imaginative enough to paint a dog accurately, straight from the official standards. How long is a neck of 'fair length', a 'fairly long' back, or a 'moderately long' tail?

Let us then admit that breed standards are not 'blueprints'. Rather they are guides to be interpreted within a broad framework.

When judging, even within this framework, one often sees a proportion of every class of Bearded Collies carrying some indefinable suggestion of Bobtails or Old English Sheepdog.

The traces are elusive. Hard to put a finger on. Even harder to put a word to. But they can be seen by a perceptive and unbiased viewer.

I usually put this type on the right hand side of my final line-up. And I make my awards from the left!

ONE

The Origin of the Bearded Collie

THE SCOTTISH BEARDED COLLIE is thought to be one of the oldest British breeds. How it came to Britain is explained by the late Professor von de Schulmack. He spoke seventeen languages and had travelled all over the world to see and study dogs and was working on a book when he was killed by the Nazis, who destroyed his work.

Professor von de Schulmack believed that the Maglomaisians had medium-sized dogs of two types, one the Spitz type and the other the long-coated sheepdog type. The Spitz type was used for hunting, the other was used as a guard dog for home and cattle. The date was about 4,000 B.C., which is borne out by the discovery of the bones of dogs of this type in north-western Europe.

The present-day type of sheepdog with the longish coat common to several countries in Europe would seem to have come from the Kommondor of the Magyars. The Magyars travelled westward from Asia Minor and possibly their original home was farther eastward still.

Groups of Magyar people travelled north-west following the village Slavonic tribes who later became the Western Slavs who in turn became the Polish nation.

In the 9th century the state of Moravia extended its power and influence over what is present-day Poland and it is from the 9th century that the lowland Polish sheepdog has been known as a pure-bred type.

About 1514 the Poles were beginning to trade with other countries and there is a record of the trading of a ship whose owner, Kazimiez Grabski, sailed from Gdansk to Scotland with grain in exchange for Scottish

The Bearded Collie

sheep. With him he had six lowland sheepdogs and this is what is written:—

'To bring unto the ship the dogs were sent to move the sheep, those that were chosen to be brought unto the ship to be separated from them that were to be left behind for there were gathered together 60 head of sheep and only 20 must come unto the ship. This the dogs did, bringing forth those chosen from out of the flock.'

Now the interesting part, according to this record, is that the sheep were good Scottish sheep, much valued by the shepherd, and that this same shepherd offered a very fine horn ram for a pair of the dogs, a deal being made for a ram and a ewe, in exchange for two bitches and one dog.

There are to be found all over Europe dogs of much the same types as the Bearded and the Polish Lowland but there are hardly any of the type outside Asia Minor to the eastward. The Bergamaschi of Italy, the Rumanian sheepdog, one of the Spanish sheepdogs and several others all seem to have come from the same origin as the Kommondor breed if not from that breed itself. It appears, on the face of it, that the dogs of the Bearded type came to Britain from the west of Europe about 2,000 B.C. and that the new blood landed in Scotland helped to form the dog we have today.

So far as our knowledge goes, it is to the Welsh King Howel Dda, who reigned early in the 10th century, that we are indebted for the first reference to the sheepdog in Britain, for in a code of laws he personally drew up, and in that part which refers to the worth of dogs, appears the following:—

'18. Whosoever possesses a cur, though it be the King, its value is fourpence.

'19. A herd dog that goes before the herd in the morning and follows them home at night is worth the best ox.'

Had the Beardie, like the Bloodhound and Greyhound,

been owned in olden times by the noblemen and gentlemen of the country, records of his ancestry and history would have been numerous, but his deeds have not been emblazoned in the records of the trial and the chase. He was the hill herd's dog and humble worker.

TWO

Description of the Bearded Collie

A VERY EARLY DESCRIPTION written long before I had heard of the breed ran as follows:—

'A big rough "tousy"-looking tyke with a coat not unlike a doormat, the texture of the hair hard and fibry and the ears hanging close to the head.'

A more poetic description is given in Alfred Ollivant's book 'Owd Bob'. This book was first published by William Heinemann Ltd. in 1898 and the first illustrated edition in 1937, which was reprinted in 1947 and 1949. It is worth trying to obtain a copy of this illustrated edition (now out of print) if only for the excellent drawings by K. F. Barker. Mr Ollivant wrote:—

'Should you, while wandering in the wild sheep land, happen on moor or in market upon a very perfect gentle knight, clothed in dark grey habit, splashed here and there with rays of moon; free by right divine of the guild of gentlemen, strenuous as a prince, lithe as a rowan, graceful as a girl, with high king carriage, motions and manners of a fairy queen, should he have a noble breadth of brow, an air of still strength born of right confidence, all unassuming; last and most unfailing test of all, should you look into two snow-clad eyes, calm, wistful, inscrutable, their soft depths clothed on with eternal sadness – yearning, as is said, for the soul that is not theirs – know then, that you look upon one of the line of the most illustrious sheepdogs of the North.'

When I first started breeding Beardies the late Mr James Garrow wrote to me as follows:—

'I have been interested in Bearded Collies all my

Description of The Bearded Collie

time. I was the only judge who used to recognize them when they came up against ordinary Rough Collies. They were kept only for work. There used to be dozens of them in the Biggar and Fife districts. There were some beautiful Beardies with a dash of tan on them. You should try to introduce it again. They later became so scarce that any breeder had to resort to crossing with the O.E. Sheepdog.

'The Beardie was essentially a worker, famed for fleetness and brains, kept by butchers, farmers, etc. They did not want coat, or a coat like a Skye Terrier that the rain would run off. The coat should not be overlong and of a raw harsh texture. They should not require daily grooming and are easily kept in condition.

'I believe it is really ignorance of the breed that made shepherds turn to the smaller Border Collie that wins at sheepdog trials. Beardies had better brains than these before they went into training.

'Have you drawn up the standard for the K.C. yet? You want to emphasize the rule on coat.'

I am afraid a number of breeders, and some judges too, do not appreciate Mr. Garrow's point about coat. Coats are now tending to become over-long, so that some dogs look like small Old English Sheepdogs, a breed that was evolved from the Bearded Collie, judging by the oil painting by Philip Reinagle (1749–1833). This looks exactly like a Beardie, brown in colour, complete with tail, only with much less coat than the Beardie seen in the show ring today.

A number of these show Beardies look very similar to the O.E. Sheepdog, Ch. Brentwood girl, born 1902 and winner of 12 Challenge Certificates and 13 reserves by 1908.

There used to be two strains of Beardies, one the Border strain which was grey and white, and the other the Highland strain, which was brown and white. But

The Bearded Collie

they are now interbred so that all dogs bred today carry the blood of both strains.

A standard of the breed was drawn up by lovers of the Beardie who formed a club in Edinburgh in 1912. This gave the height as 'dogs 20–24 inches at the shoulder, bitches rather less'. When the standard was revised by the present Bearded Collie Club in 1964 the height was lowered to 21–22 inches for dogs and 20–21 inches for bitches. I think it was a pity to lower the standard to suit the dogs (which tended to get smaller due to close breeding) rather than to breed up to the standard. There are some dogs seen in the show ring today that do not reach even the lower standard.

The following is the breed standard as recognized by the Kennel Club. It was revised from the earlier standard by the present Bearded Collie Club in 1964.

CHARACTERISTICS. The Bearded Collie should be alert, lively and self-confident. Good temperament essential.

GENERAL APPEARANCE. An active dog with long, lean body and none of the stumpiness of the Bobtail and which, though strongly made, does not look too heavy. The face should have an enquiring expression. Movement should be free and active.

HEAD AND SKULL. Broad, flat skull with the ears set high, fairly long foreface with moderate stop. Nose black, except with brown or fawn coats when brown is permitted.

EYES. To tone with coat in colour, the eyes to be set rather widely apart, big and bright. Eyebrows arched up and forward, but not long enough to obscure the eyes.

EARS. Medium size, drooping, with longish hair. Slight lift at the base denoting alertness.

Description of the Bearded Collie

MOUTH. Teeth large and white, never undershot or overshot.

NECK. Must be fair length, muscular and slightly arched.

FOREQUARTERS. Legs straight with good bone, pasterns flexible without weakness, covered with shaggy hair all round.

BODY. Fairly long, back level, with flat ribs and strong loins, ribcage both deep and long, shoulders flat, straight front essential.

HINDQUARTERS. Legs muscular at thighs, with well-bent stifles and hocks, free from exaggeration.

FEET. Oval in shape, soles well-padded, toes arched and close together, well-covered with hair including between the pads.

TAIL. Set low, should be moderately long with abundant hair or brush, carried low when the dog is quiet, with an upward swirl at the tip, carried gaily when the dog is excited, but not over the back.

COAT. Must be double, the under one soft, furry and close, the outer one harsh, strong and flat, free from wooliness or any tendency to curl. Sparse hair on the bridge of the nose, slightly longer on the sides just covering the lips. Behind this falls the beard. A moderate amount of hair under the chin, increasing in length to the chest.

COLOUR. Slate grey or reddish fawn, black, all shades of brown and sandy, with or without white Collie markings.

SIZE. Ideal height at shoulder:
Bitches – 20-21 inches. Dogs – 21-22 inches.

The Bearded Collie

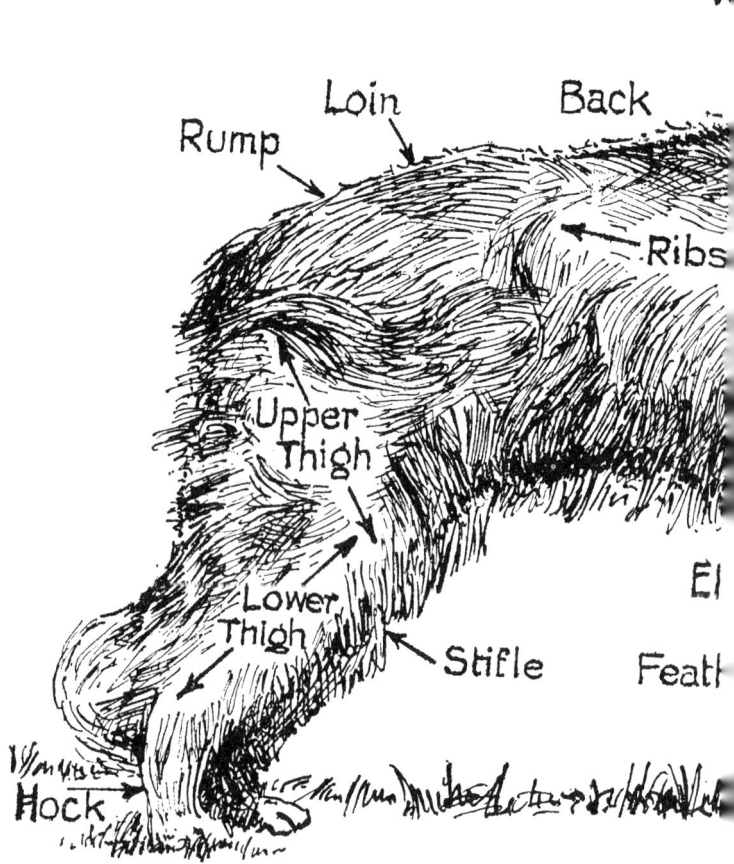

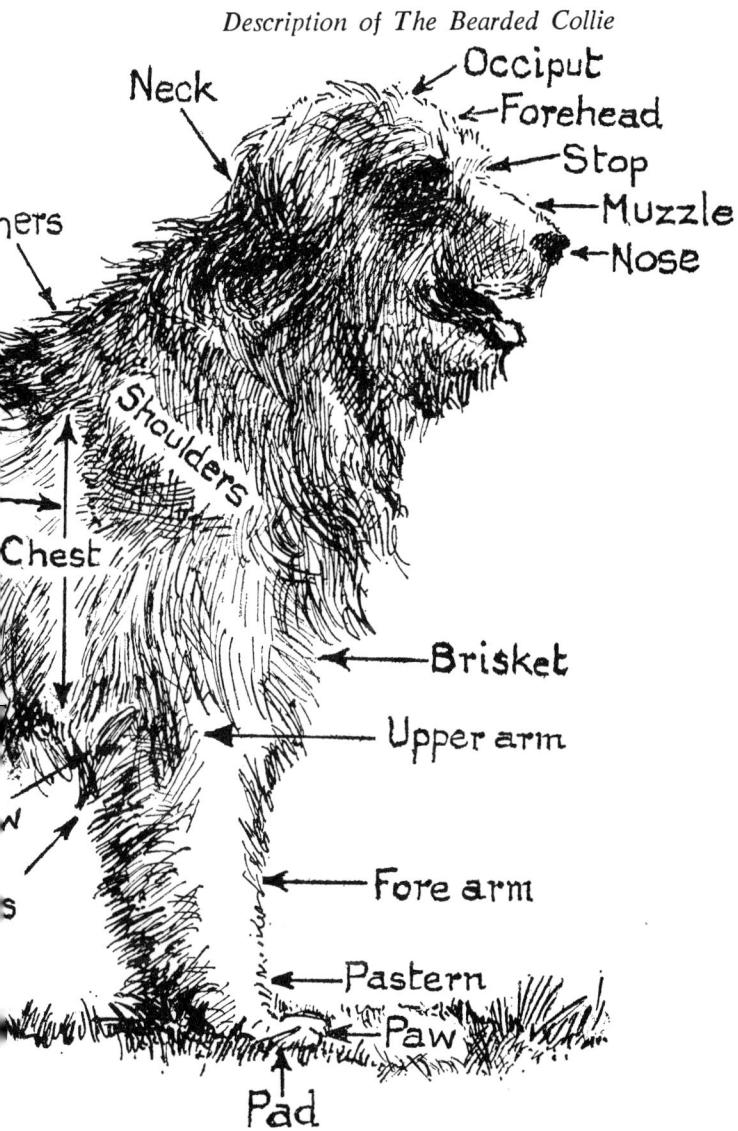

Description of The Bearded Collie

THREE

The Revival of the Bearded Collie

AS HAS BEEN stated earlier, the Beardie became extremely rare, just a few remaining belonging to shepherds and herdsmen who did not register them either at the Kennel Club or with the International Sheepdog Society, so that they were very difficult to find and were in great danger of becoming extinct.

In 1912 J. Russell Greig, C.B.E., Ph.D., M.R.C.V.S., F.R.S.E. was responsible for founding the Bearded Collie Club (or Society) in Edinburgh. The members were all very enthusiastic (Dr Russell Greig wrote) but on the outbreak of World War I their thoughts were on more serious matters and the club petered out.

In the 1930's the late Mrs Cameron Millar tried to revive interest in the Beardie. According to Mr Garrow, he found her stock for her but unfortunately they were all of one sex so she crossed them with Bobtails. 'After her death,' he said, 'they seemed to vanish into thin air.'

It was quite by chance that I took an interest in the Bearded Collie as I had never heard of the breed.

It was in January, 1944 that I decided that my next dog should be a Sheltie from working parents, and booked one from a farmers' agent. However the breeder let him down so he sent a Beardie pup sired by his own dog (though I did not learn of this until some years later).

When the chocolate-coloured fluffy baby arrived I thought she was some kind of cross-bred sheepdog, but her wonderful temperament and extraordinary intelligence so far exceeded my most optimistic hopes that I was more than satisfied.

The Revival of the Bearded Collie

It was two months later that I learned from a shepherd that she was a Bearded Collie, and though he came round to the house almost daily plaguing me to sell her to him she had, by this time, become such a beloved member of the family that no money in the world would have bought her.

This puppy was, of course, my now well-known Jeannie. She was typical of the breed that has so much personality that they become 'one of the family' rather than the family dog – a subtle but distinct difference. In fact, without human companionship Beardies would not be happy.

Jeannie was not only more lovable than any dog I had ever known but she had an uncanny intelligence and was able to herd sheep, cattle, poultry and goats without any training whatever and she demonstrated this on numerous occasions.

Although I never had thoughts of becoming a dog breeder, I felt I must find a mate for Jeannie, in order to have a future generation to carry on as my constant companion after her allotted span had taken her from us. However, had I known of the tears, heartbreaks and disappointments the attempts to reproduce another Jeannie would entail I do not think I would have had the courage to go ahead.

When Jeannie was two years old I found a local dog that looked a typical Beardie but on making inquiries about him I was told that his dam was thought to be a Border Collie. However as I did not know whether Jeannie had a known pedigree and, at that time, she was unregistered I decided to let her have a litter by him. He was a very nice dog.

In due course Jeannie whelped eight bitches and two dogs although one dog died within the hour. Jeannie was very thin at the time so I had three of the bitch puppies put down, leaving her with five bitches and one dog. They say that if you take away all but two puppies the

The Bearded Collie

bitch does not notice but settles down with the two quite happily. But no, not Jeannie. When she came in from the garden and found only six puppies instead of nine, she frantically scattered the six pups and all her bedding all over the floor in her search for the missing three. She then retired to a corner of the room thoroughly upset. She took a lot of coaxing to get her back to her babies but she did so eventually and became a most attentive mother.

All but one of the puppies were typical Bearded Collies. One – a bitch – was a Border Collie. However, after the puppies were weaned I had to go to hospital at short notice for a major operation and when I returned home I found my family had given away all the Beardie pups and left me only the Border, which I later gave to a farmer's wife.

The sire of the pups was a very old dog and he died shortly after the puppies were born, so I was unable to repeat the mating. I planned then to mate Jeannie a year later to her only son, but disappointment once again. He died of distemper only three weeks before she came in season.

When Jeannie was four years old a Collie judge saw her and told me she could get her registered at the Kennel Club. On learning this I wrote to the farmers' agent from whom I had bought her and asked him if he could give me any particulars about her breeding. He replied that she was sired by his own dog Baffler and she was bred by a Mr McKie of Killiecrankie from his bitch Mist.

After this I renewed my efforts to find a pure-bred mate for Jeannie but, in spite of advertising, press publicity and contacting farmers' agents, not one dog of known pedigree could be found.

In August 1949 a veterinary surgeon telephoned me to say that he had a beautiful Bearded Collie in his quarantine kennels and made an appointment for me

The Revival of the Bearded Collie

to meet the owner there. I was once again disappointed because although the owner maintained that he was a Bearded Collie she knew nothing about his parents and said she had had him from the time he was only three weeks old. He was, in my opinion, an undersized Old English Sheepdog with an undocked tail. She had brought him over from Canada and would later be taking him to Australia. She was very keen for me to mate Jeannie to him and wanted some of the puppies, but his head and body were definitely not typical of a Beardie.

How glad I was that I had refused this dog because about a fortnight later I went down to Brighton to visit my mother and go to the Brighton dog show. Mrs Cruft was there and I was talking to her before the show and telling her of my difficulty in finding a dog for Jeannie and she said, 'You'll be lucky soon, you'll see.'

The day after the show I went to Hove beach for a swim and in the distance I saw what looked like a Bearded Collie. I ran like a hare and when I reached him I found he was a real beauty, grey with a splendid harsh coat. I asked people nearby who the dog belonged to and was told 'the lady over there'. I immediately went to the 'lady over there' and made inquiries about the dog. She said she had bought him from the breeder, a farmer in North Devon. She had seen both parents and was able to give me the date of his birth and the name of his sire. He was $16\frac{1}{2}$ months old. I told her of my long search for a mate for Jeannie and asked if I might use him when she next came in season. Her reply was that she did not think this possible as she had moved into a flat after living in the country and she was unable to give him enough exercise and was looking for a nice country home for him. I told her that I had a nice country home with a four acre garden and would be delighted to have him.

On returning to the hotel where my mother and Mrs

The Bearded Collie

Cruft were staying I lost no time in telling them the good news. Mrs Cruft said, 'I told you you would soon be lucky. People tell me that I always bring them good luck.'

I returned home two days later with David (as the dog was called) and took him to a judge to pass for registration, after which his official name was Bailie of Bothkennar and all pedigree puppies born today are descended from him and Jeannie.

I tried to contact the breeder but he had emigrated to South Africa taking all his dogs and I was unable to trace him.

Early in February, 1950 Bailie and Jeannie were duly mated and Bailie was taken to Crufts show where he was placed third in any variety Novice (the next year he won Novice and was third in Open and the following year won the Open class with 30 entries). He was the target for press photographers being the only Beardie there (probably the first Beardie ever to appear at Crufts). Being a good showman with a sense of his own importance he posed beautifully and a few years later, when he was on television several times, he seemed to know what was required and rose to the occasion turning his head from side to side and opening and shutting his mouth, although for still cameras he always stood motionless.

On the 7th April that year the longed-for litter arrived. There were three dogs and three bitches but two of the bitches were unfortunately not up to standard. I kept the other bitch, Buskie, and the dogs, Bogle, Bruce and Bravado.

My next litter was from Jeannie mated to her only brown son Bruce and this resulted in the biggest heartbreak of all. A few days after the eight puppies were born Jeannie passed another puppy – dead. The next day my husband and I went on holiday, not knowing that this dead pup was to cause a uterine infection and

The Revival of the Bearded Collie

the milk would dry up and the pups die of starvation. I was not told at first 'in order not to spoil my holiday'. Then I had a letter from a veterinary surgeon telling me that Jeannie was 'killing her puppies'. I knew this to be untrue and telephoned my kennelmaid giving instructions for putting the pups 'on the bottle'. There were only three pups left by this time, and one was in a very bad way. But she said that they took to the artificial feeding like ducks to water and she was able to save two of them – both dogs. Jeannie continued to look after them and keep them warm and clean. Of the two survivors, one was a replica of Jeannie and the other like Bruce.

However, when they were five months old they became ill and a vet diagnosed streptococcal infection, but they became worse and almost went into convulsions with coughing. This vet still said 'they just had a cough' and gave me some cough mixture for them. So I called in a second opinion and this second vet, said immediately that it was either hardpad or distemper which was by this time too far advanced to give any chance of saving them. I not only lost all my puppies but was told that if Jeannie had another litter it might kill her. Although I longed for another try for a Bruce-Jeannie litter I decided to leave the decision to Jeannie and would only mate her if she would accept the dog willingly. She refused to let him near her.

Some years later, in June, 1958, there was born a throw-back to Jeannie. She was a granddaughter of Bruce. What a surprise and joy this was to me. She also was super-intelligent and from an early age had Jeannie's keen nose for tracking. I planned to mate her to Bravo when he was old enough, as he was the pick of the first litter to have in his pedigree the daughter and all three sons of Bailie and Jeannie. But, alas, before Bravo was old enough this lovely bitch got out and was hit by a car and although she did not seem to be badly injured

The Bearded Collie

she collapsed and died from an internal haemorrhage a few days later.

By this time I was completely involved in breeding Beardies. I would have given up when I lost Jeannie's litter by Bruce but for the fact that I had just bought Bess, a Beardie who had been working sheep in Argyll.

Bess took a dislike to Jeannie's daughter Buskie and after she had produced a litter (sired by Bogle) she became very jealous indeed and there were such savage fights that I had to part with her and gave her to a friend on breeding terms. There was only one bitch in that litter, Briery Nan.

When Nan was about five months old the Kennel Club sent Mr Clifford Owen to me to see if I would pass his dog, Newtown Blackie, for registration. This I did and also let him have Nan on breeding terms, being glad at the thought that someone else was keen to breed Beardies and hoping to get further bitch puppies from the Blackie – Nan matings. However, I was disappointed in this, as Nan's first litter contained only dog puppies and as I had a large litter by Bailie and Buskie at the time with only one bitch, Bra' Tawny, and was having difficulty selling all the dogs as the breed was still almost unknown, I took only the best pup from Nan's litter and waived my claim to a second puppy. I took the one dog in order to have a mate for Tawny later, but the poor little thing died a fortnight after I had him home and the post mortem showed that he was full of stones that he had picked up and swallowed. Therefore I used the dog that Mr Owen kept, Ridgeway Rob, when Tawny came to be mated.

Nan's second litter had only one bitch puppy and unfortunately for me Mr Owen had first choice, so I very much regretted parting with Nan, particulary as from that time he in-bred as closely as possible – father to daughter, mother to son and brother to sister, and I

An Old English Sheepdog from Vera Shaw's Book of The Dog (1880) and referred to as a "Scotch Bobtailed Sheep-dog".

Mr. H. Panmure Gordon, President of the Scottish Kennel Club, with his Beardie. From "Dog Shows and Doggy People" 1902.

"Old English Sheepdog" From an oil painting by Philip Reinagle 1749–1833 (This is reddish-fawn to White).

A Bearded Collie from "British Dogs" 1903 (Third edition).

"Scotch Colly" from Gesse's anecdotes of Dogs (1844).

Bailie of Bothkennar.

A Beardie puppy.

The Revival of the Bearded Collie

did not like the results. We have not heard of any of Mr Owen's dogs for years now.

However, Tawny produced some good puppies from her two matings to Rob. From the first litter two dogs were bought by an American lady visiting this country, she took them back with her to her farm in Connecticut. She offered me £100 each for two bitches suitable for mating with them but before such bitches became available the good lady died. Another dog from that litter became Best of Breed at Crufts before the breed had qualified for Challenge Certificates. This was Bannoch of Bothkennar who later sired my Champion Blue Bonnie.

From the second mating of Rob and Tawny Miss Partridge bought Barley and Miss Moorhouse bought Barberry and they both won their titles. By the time Barberry was one year old I had bought Britt, another outcross farm-bred dog of lovely type and temperament. Barberry was mated to him and produced ten puppies. From this litter Miss Moorhouse kept Wil o' Wisp of Willowmead who won two C.C.'s but unfortunately, owing to family reasons, Miss Moorhouse had to suspend breeding before he gained his title. Barberry was next mated to my Bobby. From this litter Miss Moorhouse retained Merrymaid of Willowmead which she subsequently mated to Wil o' Wisp. From this litter Miss Partridge bought a bitch W. My Honey who, in her turn became a champion and dam of Champions and many other prizewinners. One of these was Ch. Cairnbahn from a mating with Barley.

1956 was a good year for me as it saw the birth of three of my future champions. Baidh, a bitch from Tawny's first litter, was mated to Bravado (son of Bailie and Jeannie) and from that litter I retained Beauty Queen who won the bitch certificate and was best of breed at the first three shows at which Challenge Certificates were awarded to the breed – this was in 1959. Beauty, in her turn, produced two champions in her

The Bearded Collie

first litter. Ch. Bravo and Ch. Bosky Glen. This was the first litter to have the daughter and all three sons of Bailie and Jeannie in its pedigree. Bravo became a grand stud dog siring many champions. That same year – 1956 – I had a surprise visit from Mr Keith Hicks from a farm in Sussex. The Kennel Club had given him my name and address to see if I would pass his Beardie bitch (later registered as Jennifer of Multan) for registration. She was a beauty of good size and type and a rich reddish-sandy colour. I brought Bruce in for Mr Hicks to see and the dog immediately indicated that the bitch was in season. Mr Hicks agreed to let me keep her for mating – she was not then quite ready – and very kindly let me have pick of litter in lieu of stud fee. My choice became my Ch. Bronze Penny who was also a good size – 22 inches at the shoulder – like her dam. Penny in her turn was the dam of Ch. Benjue and, in the same litter, my lovely throw-back to Jeannie whose life was so tragically ended when she was hit by a car. Also, in this year, Bess's daughter, Bond (by Bailie) that I had sold on breeding terms was mated to an outcross dog in Scotland and my choice of puppy became my Ch. Bobby.

It was a great heartbreak in the winter of 1963–64 when I had to give up my dogs because of ill-health. I kept only Britt and Brunetta (a younger sister of Benjie who was well on the way to becoming a champion herself) and sold all my young stock. I gave away my six champions to people who would care for them as house pets and look after them in their old age. My kennel-maid had Ch. Bobby and she took a post in South Africa after leaving me. Bobby won another seven certificates there and sired champions when mated to a bitch I had sent out earlier as a puppy. My two youngest champions, Bravo and Blue Bonnie, went to Mr and Mrs Osborne in Lancashire where they continued to win certificates and bred further champions which are registered under the Osbornes' prefix of

The Revival of the Bearded Collie

DATE OF BIRTH 11 November 1962   BRED BY G. O. Willison

KENNEL NAME   OWNED BY Miss S. J. Holmes

Pedigree of Ch. Bracken Boy of Bothkennar

PARENTS	GRAND-PARENTS	G.G.-PARENTS	G.G.G.-PARENTS	G.G.G.G.-PARENTS
SIRE Ch. Bravo of Bothkennar	**SIRE** Blimber of Bothkennar	**SIRE** Balichan of Bothkennar	**SIRE** Britt of Bothkennar	**SIRE** Jock (worker)
				DAM Mootie (worker)
		DAM Bra' Tawny of Bothkennar	**SIRE** Bailie of Bothkennar
				DAM Buskie of Bothkennar
		DAM Ch. Bronze Penny of Bothkennar	**SIRE** Bruce of Bothkennar	**SIRE** Bailie of Bothkennar
				DAM Jeannie of Bothkennar
			DAM Jennifer of Multan	**SIRE** Unknown worker
				DAM Unknown worker
	DAM Ch. Beauty Queen of Bothkennar	**SIRE** Bravado of Bothkennar	**SIRE** Bailie of Bothkennar	**SIRE** Dandy (worker)
				DAM Unknown worker
			DAM Jeannie of Bothkennar	**SIRE** Baffler (worker)
				DAM Mist (worker)
		DAM Baidh of Bothkennar	**SIRE** Ridgeway Rob	**SIRE** Newtown Blackie
				DAM Briery Nan of Bothkennar
			DAM Bra' Tawny of Bothkennar	**SIRE** Bailie of Bothkennar
				DAM Buskie of Bothkennar
DAM Ch. Blue Bonnie of Bothkennar	**SIRE** Bannoch of Bothkennar	**SIRE** Ridgeway Rob	**SIRE** Newtown Blackie	**SIRE** Unknown worker
				DAM Unknown worker
			DAM Briery Nan of Bothkennar	**SIRE** Bogle of Bothkennar
				DAM Bess of Bothkennar
		DAM Bra' Tawny of Bothkennar	**SIRE** Bailie of Bothkennar	**SIRE** Jandy
				DAM Unknown
			DAM Buskie of Bothkennar	**SIRE** Bailie of Bothkennar
				DAM Jeannie of Bothkennar
	DAM Bond of Bothkennar	**SIRE** Bailie of Bothkennar	**SIRE** Dandy	**SIRE** Unknown
				DAM Unknown
			DAM unknown worker	**SIRE** Unknown worker
				DAM Unknown worker
		DAM Bess of Bothkennar	**SIRE** Bobby (worker)	**SIRE** Don (worker)
				DAM Lassie (worker)
			DAM Bett (worker)	**SIRE** Baldie (worker)
				DAM Meg (worker)

SIGNED   DATE

Published by "Our Dogs" Publishing Co. Ltd., Oxford Road Station Approach, Manchester, 1. (Copyright).

The Bearded Collie

Osmart and, for a number of years, regularly won the stud dog and brood bitch trophies. My older champions went to people who agreed to retire them from the show ring and breeding.

All the stock from which I had to build my strain of Bearded Collies were farm bred with mostly unknown, or partly known, pedigrees. The following pedigree gives a good example of line breeding as opposed to in-breeding. Bracken Boy was the latest champion I bred before having to retire from breeding. He has won at least 15 Challenge Certificates.

Many more breeders have come into the field since I retired and there are many more champions as, with the increase in registrations, many more Challenge Certificates are offered for the breed. For the first few years from 1959 only four sets of C.C.'s were available each year but by 1970 12 sets are to be won. In spite of the present numbers of champions no one else seems to have succeeded in building up their own strain.

FOUR

Buying Your First Puppy

BEFORE BOOKING YOUR first puppy (don't be surprised that most owners of champion bitches get their litters booked before they are ready to be sold – sometimes even before they are born) it is advisable to attend a few championship shows where Beardies are classified. Take a copy of the standard with you and buy a catalogue so that you can look up the breeding of the dogs that take your fancy and measure up most closely to the standard in type and temperament. The catalogue will give the names of the parents of the dogs; also the names and addresses of the breeders and/or owners.

You may find that the dogs that catch your eye may not have been bred by the owner but the breeder may have one or both parents entered for the show, as well as other dogs from the same kennel.

Ask these breeders what young stock they have for sale or expect to have in the near future. Do not ask for particulars of all their puppies, but state your requirements exactly, i.e., whether you want a dog or a bitch, and whether you want it for show and breeding, obedience training, or just a pet for the children. After you get home after the show write to the breeder of your choice making a firm booking for a puppy, once more stating your requirements in detail.

If you just want a pet, and have no wish to show or breed, it is not worthwhile to pay the price of the pick of the litter, nor will the breeder want to sell it to you, for they like their best pups to be seen in the show ring, which is a good advertisement for their kennels.

Beardies are extremely good with children and are very

The Bearded Collie

patient and forbearing when young children are over-demonstrative and treat them rather roughly. J. M. Barrie knew the breed when he chose a Beardie as Nana in Peter Pan.

If you want to visit any kennels to see the stock or to collect your puppy do please make an appointment and be sure to arrive at the appointed time. Breeders are very busy people and have to work to a strict timetable with feeding, exercising, etc. and may have gone out of their way in order to be at home and free when you are due to arrive, and perhaps postponed the dogs' walk until later. If you are an hour late this may mean the dogs missing their exercise.

If you have thoughts on becoming a breeder buy the best bitch you can afford. Sometimes a breeder will only sell his pick of litter bitch on breeding terms, i.e. half price and some of the puppies by arrangement. This may be that the breeder takes the first and third choice of the first litter and the second choice of the second litter, after which the bitch is transferred to the purchaser. The choice of stud dog is the prerogative of the breeder who is responsible for the stud fee. To buy a bitch on breeding terms has a number of advantages for anyone not very familiar with the breed, or for an inexperienced breeder, as they can reckon on getting advice and help from the breeder of the bitch in whose interest it is that the puppies should be of good quality and well-reared. They are also likely to become the owner of a good bitch – possibly a champion – which will become their own with no strings attached after two litters.

Do not be tempted to buy your own stud dog. The service of the best dog in the country can be had for less than the cost of a two-months-old puppy. If you want a stud dog wait until you have a top-notch puppy you have bred yourself and run him on to see if he makes the grade. You will, with luck, have the great pride and satisfaction of breeding your own champion dog.

Buying your first Puppy

Before you get your puppy home have a bed ready for him. You may already have one of those canvas beds standing off the ground on an iron frame with sides to keep out the draught. If not, a tea chest on its side with a four inch strip of wood tacked in front to keep in the bedding will make an excellent draught-proof bed for a two-months-old puppy, but he will soon outgrow it. Then a larger bed may be bought, one large enough for him to lie stretched out when fully grown.

Beardies are very easy to house train as they are naturally clean; of course, puppies need to be taken out in the garden to relieve themselves at more frequent intervals than adult dogs.

If you are prepared to spend the time needed to bring up the puppy as a house pet, letting him follow you from room to room and playing with him, you will be amply rewarded. Beardies thrive on human companionship and not only does this develop their innate intelligence to a high degree, but a strong bond grows between owner and dog when a puppy is brought up in this way that can never be obtained with a kennel-reared puppy.

At the time you get your pup ask the breeder if it has been wormed and whether it has had any inoculations. A 'measles' inoculation can be given at eight weeks to give temporary protection until the full inoculation is given at three months old. Until this second injection has taken effect the pup should be exercised only in the garden and should not be taken on the streets or to public parks where he might pick up infection.

FIVE

The Welfare of the Bearded Collie

THE BEARDIE IS a very energetic dog and needs plenty of exercise. He is not the kind of dog that is content with just a walk round the block or to the shops, but requires free running exercise in a large park or open fields. However, some road work is beneficial to harden the pads and keep the toe-nails short.

The coat is easily kept in condition by brushing two or three times a week with very little combing, as this takes out too much of the under-coat. However, at the time of year that the dog is shedding his coat, a comb may be used more freely and daily grooming is advisable to get rid of the loose hair so that it does not become matted. This more-frequent brushing encourages the growth of the new coat.

An adult dog needs about one pound of raw meat daily (fit for human consumption) and a bitch about three quarters of a pound. A young growing dog or bitch requires 50% more than an adult of the same weight. The meat meal is given in the early evening and a meal of porridge and milk and some hard dog biscuits is much appreciated for breakfast.

The meat should be supplemented with two level teaspoonfuls of Kenadex and two level teaspoonfuls of Stress. Also six to eight Vetzyme tablets should be given daily, either on the meat or separately as 'sweets'.

Extra meat should be given during pregnancy and up to $2\frac{1}{2}$ times as much during lactation, some of the extra meat being given at midday. Double the amount of supplements should also be given for the welfare of both the bitch and her puppies.

Britt of Bothkennar.

Ch. Bravo of Bothkennar.

Ch. Benjie of Bothkennar. Three times Best of Breed at Crufts.

Ch. Blue Bonnie of Bothkennar with one of her eight puppies by Britt.

The Welfare of the Bearded Collie

GROOMING

The Bearded Collie requires no stripping or trimming. Special mention should be made of the hair between the pads of the feet as this is a feature of the breed and should not be cut or trimmed with scissors (as with the Old English Sheepdog). A number of judges lift up the paws to make sure this hair has not been tampered with.

A Beardie should become accustomed to being brushed from puppyhood. Some pups may not take kindly to this at first but if you talk to them gently all through the grooming they soon become accustomed to it. Jeannie was a prime example of this method. In fact, during the whole of her life she refused to be groomed without a running commentary as follows: 'Lie on your back Jeannie and let me do your tum, that's a good girl.... Now sit up and let me do your chest, isn't that nice. Now give me a paw... now the other paw.... Now stand up and let me do your back' etc., etc. With this method I had her full co-operation. She positioned herself and held up her paws as requested and stayed still even when she had to be combed when shedding her coat.

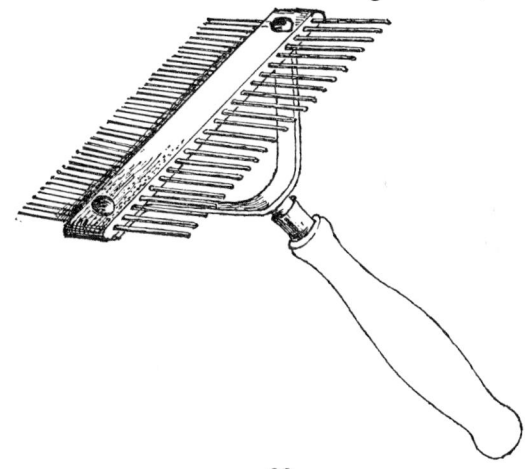

The Bearded Collie

If a Beardie is brushed two or three times a week a comb should rarely be necessary except during a moult as combing takes too much of the dense undercoat. A Hindes pin brush or any long bristle brush with the bristles not too closely spaced is used for the regular grooming. A bitch nursing a litter should be brushed every day as the puppies mess up her coat. A comb may be necessary at this time too. The comb should have widely spaced teeth also closer teeth such as Spratt's 69 (see illustration). If any tangles or mats have formed in the coat these may be teased out with the fingers and the end tooth of the coarser comb.

The Beardie should not be bathed more often than absolutely necessary. He should be bathed about a week before a show (unless he has had a recent bath for some other reason). A bitch should be bathed after she has been in season, also after she has reared a litter.

Before taking the dog to the bathroom everything must be prepared in readiness. Firstly the brush and comb must be washed, then one's own towels must be removed from the room and replaced by the dog towels, a small one to rub off the worst of the water and an old bath sheet to give the dog a good rub down. Another old bath sheet (I use a washable rug that was originally used on the floor of my babies' playpen) should be laid out in the room to be used for drying the dog, with the brush and comb and electric hair dryer laid on it in readiness.

I wear an old nylon waterproof (with the sleeves rolled up) when bathing the dogs as protection when they shake themselves which they should be encouraged to do after the final rinse. A hand shower is a most useful adjunct for the preparatory wetting also rinsing as this is much easier than constantly filling jugs of water from the taps to pour over the dogs.

As many Beardies have a very weather resisting coat it is often difficult to get the water to penetrate right through and get them thoroughly wet before applying the sham-

The Welfare of the Bearded Collie

poo. Therefore I find it much easier to apply if a three or four inch polythene bottle is half filled with the shampoo and then filled up with water.

The shampoo should be lathered in twice. After the first application has been rinsed out the second time should bring out further dirt and afterwards every bit should be thoroughly rinsed away. The back and hindquarters should be washed first, then the chest and legs leaving the head until last. Special attention should be paid to the eyes and ears so as not to get the shampoo or water in the eyes or down the canal of the ears.

When drying the dog lift up layers of the top coat with the brush to let the warm air from the dryer penetrate through the long coat to dry this and reach the dense undercoat as well.

The best shampoo to use is called 'J.D.S.' This was marketed only after intense research, mainly on Bearded Collies and Shetland Sheepdogs. In fact the letters stand for 'Jeannie Dog Shampoo'. In addition to getting the coat beautifully clean without undue softening it is also medicated and insecticidal.

During the week prior to a show the dog should be brushed daily sprinkling in grooming powder to keep the coat clean and to harden it off if it is at all softened by the bath. This grooming powder should penetrate through the coat and be thoroughly brushed out with a stiff brush.

If the dog is exercised only on grass with no walks on tarmac or playing in concrete runs the toenails will probably require cutting and filing from time to time as soft ground does not wear them down. Be careful not to cut into the quick.

If the teeth are at all discoloured they should be brushed with a solution of peroxide of hydrogen, using an ordinary toothbrush. This is sufficient for a young dog but an old one may require to have his teeth scaled. An instrument can be bought for this purpose but quite good results may be obtained by the use of the milled edge of a sixpence.

Even though the utmost care has been taken to keep the dog clean between the day of his bath and the date of the show, the weather has a nasty trick of turning wet either the day of the show or the previous day. This inevitably means that the white markings must be washed again, particularly the beard and the legs. A washing-up bowl is used for this (with the J.D.S. shampoo) starting with the beard and finishing with the feet. When almost dry more dry cleaning powder should be rubbed in and left in until arrival at the show.

Even after all this preparation fate may be against you if it is an outdoor show and the rain pours down overnight so that getting the dogs from the car park to the benches one has to wade through a quagmire of mud. All is not lost, however, if one is prepared for this. Take an aerosol can of Vetzyme Dry Foam Shampoo and a towel (or a roll of paper kitchen towels if for several dogs) to get the whites really white again after drying off the mud with cleaning powder and brushing out as much as possible. An extra brush should be brought for this purpose so that a clean one is available for the final brush up after using the dry foam shampoo.

All cleaning powder should be completely brushed out of the coat before the dog is taken into the show ring.

SIX

Preparing the Bearded Collie for Show

IT HAS OFTEN been said, not only about Beardies but about all breeds, that the novice exhibitor does not stand a chance against established breeders. This is far from true. Anyone who pays a top price for the pick of litter puppy stands a very good chance, and frequently takes home the challenge certificate, providing the dog fulfils his early promise and the owner spends the time and takes the trouble to prepare him for show in the manner of the experienced exhibitor.

On the other hand, if when buying a puppy the purchasers tell the breeders that they don't want to show, but only want a pet for the children and pay only a pet price, and decide later that they want to have a go, it is extremely unlikely that they would do well in the ring, especially if they took the dog into the ring without any preparation or training.

The Bearded Collie requires no stripping or trimming for the show ring. The most important preparation for an exhibitor is to allow him plenty of free running exercise to get him into the lean, hard condition which is natural to the breed, to teach him to move freely on a slack lead at both a walk and a trot, and to train him to stand naturally while the judge is looking at him. This training should be started well before his show debut and not left till the last week. Beardies are such friendly creatures that a youngster in the ring for the first time may forget all his lessons and try to play with the other dogs and so pull all over the place. A few sessions at obedience training classes will accustom him

The Bearded Collie

to company so that he will keep his attention on his owner.

Though the Beardie is a working dog no judge will look kindly upon him if he still has samples of the local soil clinging to his coat. Therefore give him a bath seven to ten days before the show, which will give the coat time to harden and get back into condition. After the bath rough-dry with towels and finish by brushing until completely dry. This is accomplished quite quickly out of doors on a hot sunny day, but an electric hair dryer is a useful alternative.

During the following week regular brushing is most important; also brush in dry cleaning powders (obtainable from any pet stores) to harden the coat that has been softened by bathing. On the morning of the show, or the night before, wash the feet and other white parts and when dry rub with chalk block. Most of the mud and dirt which he may pick up on the journey will brush off quite easily with the chalk. Take more chalk with you to the show, but it is important that it should be entirely brushed out of the coat before the dog enters the ring.

This takes care of the coat, but do not overlook the ears and teeth. Dogs sometimes collect dirt between the folds inside the ear which should be gently washed and carefully dried. If the teeth are at all discoloured brush them with an ordinary tooth brush dipped in hydrogen peroxide. This is sufficient for young dogs but older ones may need to have the teeth scaled. A special instrument can be bought for this but effective results can be obtained with the milled edge of a sixpence.

When giving the final brush up before entering the ring the hair on either side of the muzzle should be brushed downwards, the beard brushed forward, the hair on the top of the head brushed back and the hair on the back brushed towards the head. The natural movement of the dog will then loosen the hair so that it resumes its shaggy appearance. If the coat is the right texture

Preparing The Bearded Collie for Show

the hair above the brows should arch over the eyes, but should not fall flat over the muzzle.

The Bearded Collie should have a sharp, inquiring expression and this is impossible if the face is hidden in a mass of long hair like an Old English Sheepdog.

SEVEN

Mating and Whelping

No BITCH SHOULD be mated before she is one year old but choice of stud dog and arrangements for sending or taking the bitch to the dog should be made in advance.

For anyone inexperienced in the breed the advice of the breeder of the bitch should be sought about the choice of the dog, as he or she will have knowledge of the different bloodlines and know which stud dog is most likely to suit the bitch and produce a litter of good puppies.

Some maiden bitches have a very tough stricture which makes mating difficult and painful for them. To avoid this trouble, at about the fourth or fifth day of the season an experienced breeder or a veterinary surgeon should examine the bitch and, if necessary, dilate or break down this stricture.

The best time for mating is usually the ninth and tenth day of the season, but this can vary in individuals. I have had bitches brought to me on the eleventh day whose season was over and neither the dog nor bitch took the slightest interest in one another. They were subsequently brought on the seventh day and mated right away and had good litters. On the other hand, one bitch, brought early, would not accept the dog until the twelfth day and, although she seemed very keen, she produced only two puppies. The following year she was mated on the twenty-fourth day of her season and had a large litter.

The period of gestation is about two months, usually 63 days, but can be a few days earlier or later. A good

Mating and Whelping

whelping box can be made by any handyman (see illustration) and the bitch should be given it to sleep in several days before the litter is due to get her accustomed to it.

A piece of plywood covered with Formica should be made slightly smaller than the floor of the box so that a length of strong sacking can be placed over it and tucked underneath. When whelping is completed the wet sacking must be removed and the Formica wiped clean and dried and re-covered with clean sacking.

WHELPING BOX

Constructed of ½-inch-thick wood. The top rim should be bound by a strip of metal about 1½ inches wide, bent to shape and nailed in position to prevent the wood being gnawed.

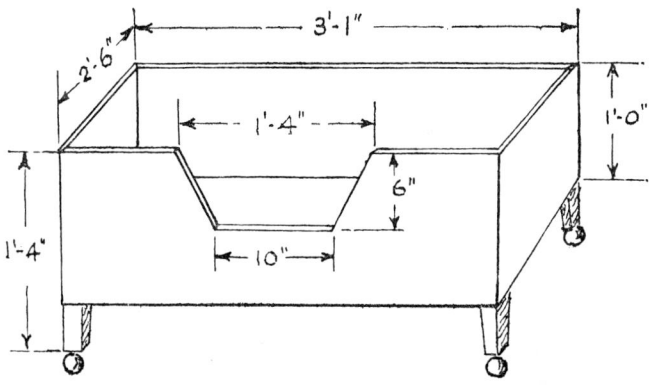

As the expectant mother likes to 'make her bed' when whelping is imminent I always covered the sacking with newspaper which she busily tore up to make a 'nest'. The paper should be removed when contractions begin. If the bitch continues straining for two hours without any result a veterinary surgeon should be called in as it is probable that a badly-placed puppy is holding things up.

As the bitch may be very busy bed-making for two or three days before whelping, or, on the other hand, the puppies may start coming with very little warning – and generally at night – I always had them in my bedroom for the 'happy event', in order to be able to stay in bed except when actually needed as 'midwife'.

I had an enclosure like a baby's playpen, but made of wire netting on a wooden frame, and to make sure that my carpet was kept clean a 'floor' of hardboard covered with newspaper was placed for it to rest on. This playpen was constructed so that a section could be opened to allow me to enter to attend to the mother and puppies.

As soon as the first puppy is born, in the event of the mother not cleaning up right away, it is necessary to break the bag over the head and mouth to enable the puppy to breathe. It will then start 'squeaking' and the mother will usually take over from there. When cleaned up the pups should be put to one of the teats. The bitch should be allowed to eat the afterbirths, but if she has a large litter these may be removed with newspaper after the later puppies if she seems to find them too much. Always watch for the afterbirths to make sure that none is retained.

If there have been no further contractions for two hours after the birth of the last puppy it is likely that whelping is over and the mother should be coaxed out of the bed and taken outside to relieve herself. While she is away the bed should be cleaned up and on her return she should be given a drink of Farex and milk sweetened with a little glucose.

During the first day after whelping the mother should be kept on a light diet, then afterwards her meat ration should be gradually increased until the pups are three weeks old, when she should be having about 2-$2\frac{1}{2}$ lbs a day, depending on the size of the litter and on her appetite.

EIGHT

Your First Litter

THE PUPPIES WILL be fed and kept clean by their mother for the first three weeks of their life.

However, between the third and fifth day they should have their dew claws removed. For the inexperienced, this should be done by a veterinary surgeon. Their other claws need to have the sharp tips cut off about once a week, otherwise the poor mother will get badly scratched. This is an easy matter that the owner can attend to, but it is helpful if someone else holds the puppy.

Weaning starts at three weeks and at this time we start training the pups in cleanliness. We had a home-made box – zinc-lined – half filled with sawdust, and every time we went to the kennel to feed them we popped them into the box both before and after the meal. By five weeks old they had learned to jump in themselves and kept their beds and kennel floor clean during the day, although it took a little longer to get them to use the box during the night. From six weeks old we took them for a run in the garden after their meat meals – weather permitting.

At the start of weaning the puppies should be getting all the milk they need from the dam and only if she is unable to satisfy them should they be given extra.

For the first few days they should have scraped meat. To scrape it do not use a knife but the thinnest dessert or tablespoon you have, as this will remove the soft meat and leave the fibres behind. For the first day or two the puppies must be hand fed, half-a-teaspoon each on the first day, increasing the amount daily (see table) until by the end of the first week they are having half-an-ounce at each meal. It can now be minced. Each puppy should have its own dish and they should be fed only two at a time so that you can ensure that each pup has its fair share. When the puppies are eating their meat readily they can be fed up to six at a time with the aid of a home-made 'dinner table' as illustrated.

PUPPY WEANING
3 weeks
BEARDIES

	NOON						5.30 p.m.		
1st day	½ teaspoon scraped meat								
2nd ,,	¾	,,	,,	,,			¾ teaspoon scraped meat		
3rd ,,	1	,,	,,	,,		1	,,	,,	,,
4th ,,	1¼	,,	,,	,,		1¼	,,	,,	,,
5th ,,	1½	,,	,,	,,		1½	,,	,,	,,
6th ,,	2	,,	,,	,,		2	,,	,,	,,
7th ,,	½ ounce minced meat						½ ounce minced meat		

4 weeks

8th day	½ oz. minced meat*						1 oz. minced meat		
9th ,,	½	,,	,,	,,	*	1 Vetzyme	1	,,	,,	,,
10th ,,	½	,,	,,	,,	*	1 ,,	1½	,,	,,	,,
11th ,,	1	,,	,,	,,	*	1 ,,	2	,,	,,	,,
12th ,,	1	,,	,,	,,	†	1 ,,	2	,,	,,	,,
13th ,,	1	,,	,,	,,	†	2 ,,	2½	,,	,,	,,
14th ,,	1	,,	,,	,,	†	2 ,,	2½	,,	,,	,,

5 weeks

15th day 1 oz. minced meat   2 Vetzyme   3 oz. minced meat

* Dam with pups at 10 a.m. and 3 p.m. for 20 minutes.
† Dam with pups at night only.

Dam at night only for a few more days, then 8 a.m. feed of porridge and milk increasing meat as required – 2 ounces midday and all other increases at 5.30. Pups should reach 6 ounces a day by beginning of 7th week. Farex and milk given at bed-time from start of 6th week.

Your first Litter

'PUPPIES' DINNER TABLE'

Base 18½ inches x 14½ inches, ¼ inch x 3 plywood.

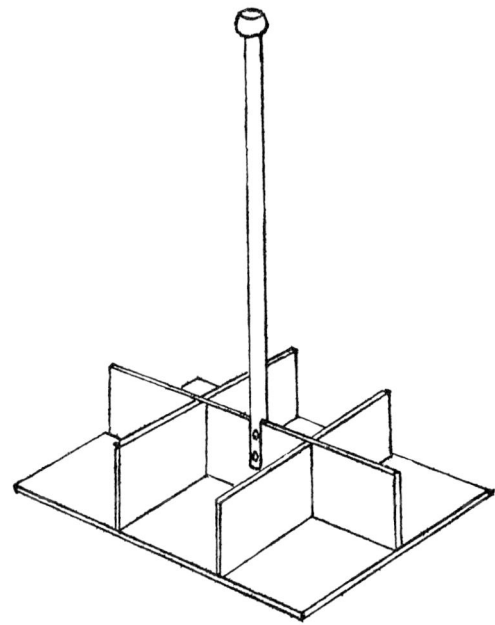

At the age of 5½ weeks the dam should no longer sleep with the pups at night, but for a few more days she should be allowed in with them for about 15 minutes after they have had their late supper of Farex, glucose and milk. At this age they should have the supplements on their evening meal with ½ a teaspoon of Kenadex and ½ a saltspoon of Stress, increasing to 1¼ teaspoons of Kenadex and ¾ teaspoon of Stress at two months. At this age the amount of meat should have gradually increased to 2 ounces at noon and 5 ounces in the evening (about 5 – 5.30) and about 6 Vetzyme tablets daily.

The Bearded Collie

The amount of meat recommended is only a rough guide. Give only the amount the pups will eat up readily. Some litters get ahead of schedule while others lag a few days behind.

The meat and supplements should be increased weekly so that at the age of five months a puppy should have the same amount as an adult and at nine months 50% more.

The puppies should be ready to go to their new homes at eight weeks if the buyer is coming to fetch them but should be nearer nine weeks if sent by rail. Before they are sold all puppies should be wormed, even if the dam is wormed three weeks after mating. The best time for worming is when they are six weeks old and a further dose a week later. If worming tablets are obtained from the veterinary surgeon he will give instructions as to dosage. This may vary with different makes of tablets.

NINE

The Stud Dog

IF YOU SHOULD take up breeding seriously you will probably, sooner or later, have your own stud dog and, if he is a good one, you will have to cope with visiting bitches.

Have the bitch in a safe run, kennel or room where there is space for the dog and bitch to frisk around. One way of telling when a bitch is ready is to stroke her back from the shoulder to the tail. If she wraps her tail round against her side the dog can be taken to her – on a lead at first, in case he is overkeen and rushes her too much.

It takes two people to assist in a successful mating. One to hold the bitch's collar (which should be tightened for the occasion to make sure she does not slip it). I found the best way was to put the thumbs through the collar on each side of the neck, thus keeping the fingers free to keep the head steady so that she does not turn round and snap at the dog when he mounts her.

The other, and more experienced, person should sit on the left-hand side of the bitch and have her left hand underneath the bitch's rear end with the fingers towards the vulva to make sure she does not sit down at the critical moment; also to ensure that the dog's penis is in the vagina when he starts working and that he does not spend himself between her legs. When you are sure the dog's penis has penetrated and he is working rapidly the right arm can be passed behind him (if it does not put him off) to steady him and hold him firmly until the 'tie' has taken place. Many dogs would prefer to 'get on with the job' unaided but if you can accustom them to

The Bearded Collie

accept this assistance it is a great help when difficult bitches have to be mated.

Some bitches, even experienced ones, whimper a lot during the initial stages of mating, but once the tie has been completed they generally quieten down.

At the completion of the tie, when the dog has stopped working, he should be held steady for a few moments and when he shows signs of wanting to turn he should be assisted in this very gently, slowly helping one leg over the bitch's back and when they are standing back to back the two tails should be held together firmly at the base – the first assistant still keeping a hold on the bitch's collar. A tie can last anything from two minutes to one hour and a single mating is usually sufficient, except with the first mating of a young dog when a second mating should be given as the semen from the first mating may be dead. This is not always the case – there are exceptions to every rule – and my dog Britt had his first mating (with no second mating) to Barberry when they were both eleven months old and she produced ten healthy puppies.

After the mating we always wiped those parts of the dog that had come in contact with the bitch's hindquarters with cotton wool dipped in a solution of Dettol and water. This was not only for the sake of hygiene but also not to excite the other dogs.

Chs. Benjie and Bravo of Bothkennar. Crufts Best of Breed winners.

Jeannie of Bothkennar.

Ch. Beauty Queen of Bothkennar. The first British Bearded Collie Champion.

TEN

Colour in Beardies

THE MAJORITY OF Beardies are born black and turn grey when they get their adult coat. This grey may be almost black or quite a silvery grey or any shade in between. The reason so many are born black is because this is the dominant colour. A Beardie born blue, brown or fawn has to receive the gene for these colours from both his parents, otherwise the black will prevail. The white Collie markings may be slight or may be as much as the entire legs, muzzle and part or full collar and, of course, the tip of the tail.

For the purpose of clarity I shall in this chapter refer to the colour at birth, regardless of the shade of grey, brown or reddish-fawn the dogs become when adult.

Two browns mated together cannot produce any black puppies as they are pure for brown, having received the gene for this colour from both parents. But two blacks mated together can produce brown puppies if they carry the gene for brown and this is passed on by both of them in any one puppy. However, if two browns are mated together (unless they are really dark, which is rare) they are apt to produce pale fawns which sometimes turn off-white, with light pigmentation. It is better to mate a brown bitch with a black dog that has brown in his near ancestors if you want some brown puppies. A blue bitch should also be mated to a black. There is nothing against mating two blacks.

One rather strange phenomenon I found was that the blacks were far more resistant to infection than the other colours. Jeannie, a reddish-brown, had distemper when she was young but recovered. Her two brown sons died

The Bearded Collie

of it owing to wrong diagnosis and I had a blue and a fawn who had it and recovered. We had no other dogs when Jeannie had the infection but with the later ones it was not caught by any of the blacks.

A more striking example of the black's resistance to infection was one year, just after Christmas, when one of my Shetland Sheepdogs went down with gastro-enteritis (or dog 'flu). Then a brown Beardie became affected and then another Sheltie. (The Shelties were all sable and white.) I was afraid this might go on for weeks and prevent me being clear of infection in time to send in my Crufts entry, so I put all the dogs together in the dog room to get it over as quickly as possible. The only exceptions were my two 'old age pensioners' Bailie (black) and Bruce (brown) who were kept in our living room, and two nine-weeks-old puppies (the rest of the litter having been sold), Bravo (black) and his litter sister (brown) which I was keeping for another three weeks as she was to be exported to Thailand.

In spite of all the vomiting and diarrhoea in the 'sick bay' not one of the black dogs caught the infection although all the browns and the Shelties had it. And, in spite of the isolation, Bruce had it and so did the brown puppy. Bailie remained free; so did the black puppy, even although he remained with his sister all the time she was ill.

We had a pretty hectic ten days cleaning up the floors and dosing the dogs but we got it over quickly and soon had a clean bill of health from the veterinary surgeon.

ELEVEN

First Aid in the Kennel

ALTHOUGH BEARDIES ARE very hardy, a first aid cupboard or chest should be kept in readiness in case of accidents or emergencies. I found a cosmetic tray very handy for keeping the following items all together:–
Veterinary thermometer
2 oz packet of cotton wool
small packet of gauze
scissors (rounded)
1 inch and 2 inch packets of Prestoband (which sticks to itself but not to the dog's fur)

The tray should be covered with a plastic bag. If you do not have one large enough to keep out the dust two may be used – one at each end and overlapping in the middle.

Also needed will be a bowl about the size of a pudding basin and a bottle of antiseptic such as Dettol for bathing cuts and bites. If a bite is really deep a veterinary surgeon should be asked for a tube of penicillin ointment to squeeze into the wound in case of bacteria, as if it is allowed to heal on the outside while infected below the surface an abscess is likely to form.

If a dog vomits and/or has diarrhoea his temperature should be taken. The dog should be lying on his side, the tail lifted and the thermometer gently inserted in the rectum. Do not use force, but if any difficulty is found grease the tip of the thermometer with vaseline and try a different angle. The thermometer should be inserted to about half its length and left in for one minute. The normal temperature should be 101.5 and you will find this marked 'Dog' on a veterinary thermometer. If the

The Bearded Collie

temperature is normal or only 102 a day's starvation with just a little milk and glucose will probably have the dog back right as rain by the next day. However, if the trouble continues beyond one day or if the dog has a high temperature the veterinary surgeon should be called in as it may be the first symptom of something more serious. Any dog so affected should be kept isolated from the rest of the kennel.

FLEAS AND LICE. Most dogs – particularly country dogs – have unwelcome parasites at some time in their lives and it is necessary to get rid of them as soon as they are noticed. The flea is the host of the tape-worm egg. Prevention and treatment are the same. Dust the whole dog with one of the Gammexene powders, making sure it gets through to the undercoat. The bedding and cracks in the floorboards should also be dusted with the powder.

Another effective method is to place the dog in a large washtub or baby's bath and mix up some Kurmange (obtainable at pet stores) with water and pour it over and over the dog until he is completely saturated. Then, after he has given himself a good shake, take him for a brisk run until he is dry. This solution should *not* be rinsed off.

TICKS. Dogs in contact with sheep or cattle are likely at times to pick up ticks. These fasten on to the dog. When they are seen do not pull them off or the head will remain and cause a nasty sore. Put a drop of methylated spirit round the head of the tick and after a few moments try to ease it off gently with tweezers. If it will not come off by this method it is better to leave it to fall off in its own time.

CAR SICKNESS. This is a trouble which I have found is easier to prevent than to cure. If puppies are sick (as many of them are) when they are taken out in the car they will associate the car with sickness and will expect to be sick and a bad habit will be formed. However,

First Aid in the Kennel

if during their puppyhood they can be prevented from being sick they will outgrow it as they grow older and get used to travelling.

I have found that the best thing for preventing car sickness is Avomine (obtainable only on prescription). To start with, one tablet should be given two hours before the journey and a second one ¾ of an hour before leaving. These tablets do not make the dog dull or sleepy in any way, but with a settled tummy they keep bright and happy. As they get older and accustomed to travelling the dose may be reduced to one tablet given an hour before the start of the journey and eventually left off altogether.

THUNDERSTORMS. Some Beardies do not mind thunderstorms at all, while others pant and tremble from the time they hear the first distant rumble. Those dogs that are upset should be taken into the house and kept apart from those that have no fear, or they may transmit their fear to them. During a severe storm the dogs that are frightened may be saved a lot of distress by being given a tranquiliser. I have found Oblivon capsules very effective. These can only be obtained on prescription.

DOSING THE DOG. Giving pills is comparatively easy. It is just necessary to place the pill on the back of the tongue and hold the mouth shut until the dog has swallowed. For giving liquids a medicinal spoon with lines marking teaspoon, dessertspoon and tablespoon will be found most useful bearing in mind, now we have gone metric, that 5 ml equals one teaspoon and 10 ml equals one dessertspoon, as nearly as possible.

TWELVE

Selling Your Stock and Exporting

THE NOVICE BREEDER who does not exhibit may not find it easy to sell his puppies as he or she will not be known. Sometimes the owner of the sire or the breeder of the bitch, who has more demands for puppies than he can fulfil may buy in part of the litter. If this is the case, remember that he will expect to make a profit on the deal and may want to register them under his own kennel name. For the remainder of the litter for which there are no bookings there is left only the 'pet' market and, alas, at only 'pet' prices, but it is better to sell them at 8-9 weeks old when they are looking their loveliest than to keep them on, at considerable expense in food, until they are several months old, when they will probably fetch no more than at eight weeks.

But a novice who does well in the show ring and mates his bitch to a dog known to produce good stock should be able to sell his puppies at a reasonable price. The price quoted should be for the puppy, with the freight charges extra if it is to be sent by rail or air.

When inquiries come from abroad only the top quality puppies should be offered. No one will want to pay the high freight charges for a second-rate puppy which is unlikely to be a credit to its new owner or to the breeder. Overseas buyers expect to import stock which will become champions and breed good stock in the future.

Dogs that are to be sent abroad must have a three-generation export pedigree from the Kennel Club. (When applying for this, if the dog is a male, a certificate should be enclosed stating that the dog is entire, i.e. that both testicles have descended into the scrotum. Beardies,

Selling your stock and Exporting

unlike some other breeds, can be felt to be entire at an early age, usually about eight weeks old. The certificates may be obtained free from the Kennel Club and must be signed by a veterinary surgeon.) The K.C. pedigree and veterinary expenses can be legitimately added to the cost of the puppy; also the charges of the agent employed to arrange for the export of the dog.

It is essential for anyone without experience of exporting their stock to employ one of these agents as the rules and regulations differ from country to country, and they can tell you of the varying formalities that have to be gone through for each country. For instance, continental judges may pay great attention to teeth. As in this country, the dog should have a 'scissor bite'; i.e. the lower incisors should fit closely behind the upper incisors leaving no space between. Also, if the pre-molars are missing, the dog will be disqualified from the show ring and will be unable to be shown again. The pre-molars are the first double teeth behind the canines. If they cannot be seen in a puppy he may be X-rayed to find out if they are in the gums and will grow through as the puppy gets older.

The agents can also supply a travelling box, book flights and arrange to collect the puppy either from the breeder (if he lives near an airport) or from one of the British Rail terminals and transport it to the airport and book it in.

Do not quote a price for a puppy higher than you would do to anyone in this country. The importer will have very heavy freight charges in addition to the other expenses and bear in mind that champions in other countries bearing your prefix will be a good advertisement for your kennel and will probably lead to further orders for good stock.

THIRTEEN

Bearded Collie Clubs

THERE ARE BEARDED Collie Clubs in Britain, Holland, the U.S.A. and Canada, and everyone interested in the breed would be well advised to join the one in their own country.

I founded the Bearded Collie Club in this country in 1955 with the help of the few Beardie owners and other 'doggy' people who, though not owning a Beardie, were keen to see this old breed revived and gave me their full support by becoming founder members. These included such well-known people as the late Mr Jimmie Garrow, Miss Clara Bowring and the late Mr Frank Williams and family.

I must pay tribute to Miss Doris Lowe, who was for many years the club treasurer and secretary and who helped to build up the club to the flourishing concern it is today. We held the first club show in 1959, including classes for Rough and Smooth Collies as, at that time, there were insufficient Beardie exhibitors to make a good entry. However, after a few years the Beardie entry increased and now it is exclusively our breed, with very large entries in all classes.

The present secretary is Mrs Wendy Boorer, 34 Milton Park, London, N.6 and she is as enthusiastic as Miss Lowe, and puts in equally hard work.

The modest subscription includes free copies of the Bearded Collie Club News – a magazine that is sent to members twice a year. It is full of Beardie news and informative articles, and members are able to advertise their stock and dogs at stud. The American club is even

Bearded Collie Clubs

more ambitious as they aim to produce their News quarterly.

At the time of going to press The Bearded Collie is not recognized by the U.S. Kennel Club, as they require 300 registrations widely scattered over different parts of the country, but with 100 there already it should not be long before they breed them up to the required number.

FOURTEEN

The Kennel Club

IN ORDER TO be able to enter a dog for a show (with the exception of exemption shows) it is necessary for it to be registered at the Kennel Club and, in the case of a dog not bred by the owner, it must be transferred to the new owner. The registration and transfer forms can be obtained free from the Kennel Club. The breeder who registers the puppy will have to sign the transfer form at the time of the sale.

Anyone taking up breeding should register their own prefix for their homebred puppies, so that all their dogs can be identified as coming from their kennel. It is necessary to apply to the Kennel Club for a special form for this. Do not leave the application until you are ready to register your puppies as, with so many prefixes and affixes, it may take a little time to find one that has not already been used. All names suggested (and not already in use) are published in the Kennel Gazette so that anyone with a prefix almost the same may object if they think it will lead to confusion.

Breeding terms agreements may be registered at the Kennel Club. A specimen form is reproduced here.

CHALLENGE CERTIFICATES

These are awarded only at Championship shows and the number of these awarded annually for each breed depends on the number of registrations in the previous year. When a dog has won three challenge certificates under three different judges he can claim the coveted title of Champion.

Before entering your young hopeful at a Championship show it is a good idea to enter him in a Limited or Sanction show. It will not be so crowded and noisy for

The Kennel Club

REGISTRATION OF THE LOAN OR USE OF A BITCH FOR BREEDING PURPOSES.

FEE 20/-

Please read the Regulations and Notes overleaf before completing the Form.

Please write in ink and all Names (except Signatures) in CAPITAL letters.

I, ... (name of registered owner)
of ....
at this date the registered owner of the .... (breed)
registered at the Kennel Club under the name..
Regn. No. ....hereby give notice that I have made an arrangement
with Mr./Mrs./Miss ....
of ....
in regard to the breeding from the said bitch in future and we have agreed that the undermentioned particulars are correct, that we shall abide by the conditions below, by the Rules of the Kennel Club and the Regulations for the Loan or Use of a Bitch and that **no sale or transfer of the said bitch shall take place during the continuance of this agreement.** The breeder of all puppies is to be
Mr./Mrs./Miss .... (see note 4)
as from .... to .... (see note 5)
In order that a record be in existence governing the mating arrangements and the disposal of puppies it is advised that those conditions be entered hereunder, and if no conditions are given it will be held that all puppies belong to the breeder.

....
....
....
....
....
....

Dated ....   Signed ....

                                                                                   Signed ....

| This space for Kennel Club use only. | Return one copy of this form together with the fee to
THE SECRETARY,
THE KENNEL CLUB,
1, CLARGES STREET,
PICCADILLY,
LONDON, W.1. |

The Bearded Collie

one thing, and it will give both owner and dog experience in the show ring. A Limited show is confined to the promoting club or society and the number of classes is restricted. A Sanction show is restricted to not more than 20 classes. No dog that has won a challenge certificate is eligible so the competition is not so keen. At an Open show champions may be entered but no challenge certificates are awarded.

Crufts is the most important show of the year and is held early in February. Only dogs that have qualified may be entered. The qualifications are that the dog is already a champion or has won a challenge certificate, or has won a first prize in a breed class at a championship show since the first of January in the preceding year.

In addition to breed classes, dogs may also compete in obedience shows. A dog of a breed not on the K.C. register such as a Border Collie, a working Collie or even a cross-bred may be entered on the Obedience Record and may then be entered for obedience classes and working trials. The obedience classes at Crufts are by invitation only for dogs that have won an obedience certificate during the preceding year.

FIFTEEN

Early Training for a Young Puppy

I NEVER START OBEDIENCE training, as it is taught in classes, until the puppy is at least four months old. However, preliminary training can be started very much earlier. All puppies should have some training so that they grow up into obedient and well-behaved dogs, even although the owner does not intend competing at obedience shows. These shows are much more fun than breed shows and Beardies train readily and enjoy the competition.

Miss J. Cooke has the honour of making up the first Bearded Collie Obedience Champion with her bitch 'Scapa' (by Ch. Bosky Glen of Bothkenmar ex Swalehall Martha Scrope) and many more have won, and are currently winning, first prizes for obedience.

For the rapid house-training of the pup in its new home VIGILANCE is the key-word. Watch him carefully and always TAKE him out immediately after a meal and on waking from a sleep or at any time he seems restless and walks round in circles sniffing the floor. Run to the door calling 'Outside' and ALWAYS ACCOMPANY him and praise him when he has done what is required. Take him to the same place each time – a shrubbery is best, then the lawn and paths are kept clean and tidy. He will soon learn to run to the door when he wants to go out.

We talk to our puppies a lot so that they get to know the sound of our voices. At first it is just a jumble of sounds to them but in a short time they will learn to understand the meaning of words providing they are given singly such as 'No', '*Good* Boy'.

The Bearded Collie

In preparation for obedience training proper, I teach the puppy the words I will be using later for the Novice exercises, making sure that only *pleasant associations* are planted in the mind of the puppy with each word or action.

I first teach the word 'Come' and when he reaches me I gently stroke him into the sitting position (saying 'Sit') and then give him lots of praise, and pet him. This praise is usually sufficient for most puppies but with the difficult ones the added inducement of a tit-bit may be necessary at first. Even if the puppy is 'playing-up' he must still be praised and rewarded when he eventually comes in, in order to keep up the pleasant associations. If he is scolded, the next time he plays up he may be afraid to come, remembering his previous scolding. I start the 'Come' and 'Sit' at about eight weeks old, when he is running about the garden with me.

After the 'Come Sit' I teach the 'Heel Sit' and when the puppy is quite familiar with this position I take one step forward and with my left hand coax the puppy to move forward with me and sit again, still at my left side.

For the 'Stay' exercises I place the pup in the correct position and kneel or sit beside him saying 'Sit . . . Stay . . . Good boy', stroking his head. For the 'Down' I stroke his side or tummy. Later on I stand beside him, then walk round him, and eventually I can walk a few steps away.

At the start none of these 'lessons' lasts more than about 15 seconds, though they may be given several times a day. Each one is given separately. I wait till the pup is four months old before I combine the 'Sit . . . Stay' with the 'Come . . . Sit' and 'Heel . . . Sit' for the novice recall and finish.

To train the dog to keep closely to heel I graduate *slowly* from the one step forward to one step at a slight angle, then two, three and four steps and right and left

Early Training for a Young Puppy

turns, with my left hand at the left side of his head and neck when necessary. I find this far better than teaching Heel on lead as the pup learns from the start that his head should be right up beside the owner's left leg. With a very high-spirited dog that wants its own way it is sometimes necessary to put him on a lead to begin with, though I have found that I can never get really good heel work until the lead can be dispensed with and the dog learns that it is *his* job to keep close to me and not my job to pull him in with the lead.

This preliminary training should be given in one's home or garden, with nothing to distract the puppy's attention from the trainer. It requires patience and understanding and, above all, EVERYTHING A PUPPY IS TAUGHT MUST BE WELL WITHIN HIS CAPABILITIES, SO THAT HE CAN FEEL PROUD OF HIS ACHIEVEMENTS WITHOUT ANY SENSE OF STRAIN. If he looks forward to his lessons as a little 'treat' he will start his more serious training in the right frame of mind, eager to learn more and to do well.

Although I usually advise leaving the 'Retrieve' until the puppy is six months old – particularly with those dogs that are inclined to be difficult over this exercise – a very keen puppy may be started earlier, providing he is not allowed to do it when he has any loose teeth or tender gums during teething.

I never teach the retrieve as a game, as this often leads to trouble. The most likely consequences of this method are that the dog, when taking part in a competition, either decides he doesn't want to play or else goes to the opposite extreme and has a rare old game with the dumb-bell and refuses to bring it back to its owner.

The surest method is to teach the delivery first and, by stages, work back to the actual retrieve. First get the dog sitting squarely in front of you and put the dumb-bell in his mouth. Stroke him under the chin to prevent

The Bearded Collie

him dropping it and say firmly 'Hold it' and praise him for doing so. Then with the command 'Give' allow him to give up the dumb-bell into your hand and reward him with a tit-bit and lots of praise. At first it may be necessary to open the mouth with the thumb and forefinger to insert the dumb-bell but with the thought of the tit-bit to follow he will soon take it quite readily.

The next steps are to stroke the top of his head instead of his chin, saying firmly 'Hold it' if he shows any sign of letting it drop, and also to walk a pace or two backwards encouraging the dog to walk forwards while still holding the dumb-bell. When the dog will do this and hold on till the command 'Give' he has learned half the exercise and merits lots of praise and a really tasty reward.

When the dog has learned to hold and carry the dumb-bell the next step is to get him to pick it up off the ground. Gradually lower the hand holding the 'bell' so that he has to put his head down to take it. When he will do this throw it just two or three feet in front of you and encourage him to go for it *immediately* and bring it back. (It is easy enough to teach him to wait for a command after he has become keen.)

Occasionally one finds a dog that refuses to leave his owner's side. When this happens I have found the best method is to put him on a lead, throw the dumb-bell a fair distance and run up with him. When he has picked it up (with or without help) run back slightly ahead of him with the lead (or slip chain) under the dump-bell to prevent it falling from his mouth.

Training creates a great bond between owner and dog and, if given regularly, is very worth-while as well as being most enjoyable.

KENNEL CLUB FEES
ON AND AFTER 15th FEBRUARY, 1971

Registration by Breeder	25p
Registration by any person other than the breeder	£1.00
Registration (Breeder's declaration not signed)	£2.00
Registration Obedience Record	£1.00
Registration Name not changeable (additional) fee)	50p
Re-registration	£1.00
Transfer	50p
Loan or use of bitch	£1.00
Change of name	£5.00
Pedigrees—3 generations	£2.00
Pedigrees—5 generations	£5.00
Pedigrees—Export	£2.50
List of Wins (entered in Stud Book) ...	50p
Registration of Prefix	£3.00
Prefix Maintenance Fee	£1.00
Holders of Prefixes may compound on the payment of	£7.00
Assumed Name	£2.00
Registration of Title	£1.00
Maintenance of Title	£1.00
Formation of a Branch by a Registered Society	50p
Maintenance of Title of a Branch of a Registered Society	25p
Registration of Title of Dog Training Club	50p
Maintenance of Title of Dog Training Club	25p
For Championship, Open, Limited and Sanction Shows held under Kennel Club Rules:—	
Licence to hold the Show	75p
The following Extra Fees are payable for Championship and Open Shows:—	

Extra Fee payable up to 250 Exhibits	£1.00
Extra Fee payable for each 250 Exhibits (or part) up to 1,000	50p
Extra Fee payable for each 500 Exhibits (or part) over 1,000	50p
For permission to hold Matches under Kennel Club Regulations	50p
For permission to hold an Inter-Club Obedience Match	50p
For permission to hold an Exemption Show	50p
For permission to hold an Obedience Show at a Championship Show	75p
For permission to hold an Obedience Show at a Licence Show	75p
For permission to hold an Obedience Show at a Sanction Show	75p
For permission to hold an Obedience Show as a separate event under Licence Show Regulations	75p
For permission to hold an Obedience Show as a separate event under Sanction Show Regulations	75p
For Working Trials held under Kennel Club Rules:	
Championship Working Trials	£3.00
Open Working Trials	£2.00
Members' Working Trials	£1.00